Original title:
Puns from Pluto

Copyright © 2025 Creative Arts Management OÜ
All rights reserved.

Author: Nash Everly
ISBN HARDBACK: 978-1-80567-846-5
ISBN PAPERBACK: 978-1-80567-967-7

Orbital Humor Spectrum

In the cosmos where comets spin,
Jokes collide and laughter begins.
Stars wink with jest, bright and bold,
As meteors shower tales to be told.

Galaxies twirl, with punchlines to share,
Even the asteroids stop for a glare.
Cosmic giggles float through the night,
While Saturn rings in pure delight.

Uranus chuckles, a cheeky delight,
With one-liners that take off in flight.
Planets align for a comedy show,
Where the space-time fabric starts to glow.

A nebula bursts with colors so bright,
Sprinkling humor in the cosmic light.
In this realm, laughter is king,
As the universe dances and starts to sing.

Astro Amusements

In a galaxy far, where comets collide,
Stars twinkle bright, their laughter can't hide.
Planets spin round with a wobbly gait,
Even black holes joke, they just can't relate.

Rockets that zoom with a burst of delight,
Space cows tell tales while munching on light.
Galactic giggles flicker in flight,
While aliens chuckle through the peaceful night.

Understanding the Unseen Laughs

Nebulas form in a colorful dance,
As spacetime bends, they leap and prance.
The moons play tricks with their shadowy guise,
And meteors wink with mischievous eyes.

Gravity's pull can't dampen a jest,
As aliens gather for their pun-laden fest.
They orbit around with a glee so profound,
In the laughter of stardust, joy is unbound.

Space Odyssey of Smiles

Stars sparkle down in a cosmic parade,
Every wink from the sun, a bright escapade.
With each shooting star, a wish slips through,
For space is a theater, where dreams come true.

Quasars roar with a laugh, oh so bold,
Spinning yarns of adventures from days of old.
In the swirls of the cosmos, humor's the key,
In the embrace of the universe, we're all meant to be.

Comedic Curiosities

Asteroids dance in a jovial spin,
While the moons crack up, it's a real win-win.
Rocket jokes fly with the speed of light,
Tickling boundaries of day and night.

Galaxies collide in a comical twist,
As constellations form a humorous list.
Even the void seems to chuckle and sigh,
In the cosmic theater, laughter will fly.

Celestial Smirks

In the vast night sky, stars wink with glee,
Cosmic jokes float by, oh what a spree!
A comet zips past with a taunting grin,
While planets trade quips, where to begin?

Jupiter laughs with a thunderous roar,
While Mercury quips, 'I'm quick to the core!'
Saturn spins tales with its ringed delight,
While Martians chuckle in their red twilight.

Echoes of Earth's Humor

On Earth they make sense, but in space, who knows?
A galaxy giggles as the humor grows.
'Why did the star jump? Was it feeling bright?'
'It fell to the moon, what a silly sight!'

Earth's laughter echoes, it travels quite far,
Tickling the comets, each quip is a star.
'What do you call space with an echoing cheer?
A vacant void that's filled with jeer!'

Rising Humor Waves

Like waves that roll in on a sandy shore,
Jokes ride the rhythm, returning for more.
The sun plays tricks as it hides in the mist,
While the tide shares tales that you can't resist.

Listen to Neptune in a playful mood,
It swirls up laughter like a bountiful food.
The dolphins dive deep, splashing with flair,
Their playful antics are beyond compare!

Galaxy of Glee

In a galaxy spun with laughter and light,
Every star dances, a dazzling sight.
The meteors zoom, with a gleeful cheer,
'Catch me if you can, I'm dashing, my dear!'

Cosmic jesters drift on a shimmering breeze,
Whispering jokes among swirling trees.
In the depths of the cosmos, joy's on display,
A universe bursting with funny ballet.

Laughter Across Light Years

In the void where planets jest,
Stars exchange their cosmic best.
Asteroids giggle, orbits laugh,
While space dust sparkles like a craft.

Neptune's winds blow jokes so bold,
Mercury's tales are never old.
In this dance of moons and sun,
Galaxies unite, all in fun.

Solar Smiles

The sun grins with a radiant spark,
While moons make shadows, light up the dark.
With every comet's tail that glows,
Galactic chuckles ripple, who knows?

Venus winks and Mars gives a nod,
Earth joins in, feeling quite awed.
In this stellar ballet of mirth,
Laughter expands beyond the Earth.

Comet's Clever Quips

A comet zips with a wink and a grin,
Zooming through skies, adventures begin.
Its tail trails tales, both witty and bright,
Telling of life with a cosmic light.

Asteroids chuckle, their paths intertwined,
Each twist and turn so carefully timed.
In this endless void, they spin and glide,
With humor that's boundless, they take pride.

Cosmic Cosmic Ironies

In the vastness, irony flies,
Planets stuck in their own goodbyes.
While black holes pull with a hungry sigh,
Stars beam down with a twinkling eye.

Saturn's rings boast their style and flair,
Yet, here they spin without a care.
In the fabric of space where we all connect,
Laughter survives, what did you expect?

Comedic Nebulas

In a cloud of gas, a joke unfurled,
Stars giggled softly, bright as pearls.
Cosmic chuckles drift on high,
While planets laugh and comets sigh.

A black hole's punchline pulled you in,
Absorbing laughter, where to begin?
Galaxies spin with a twinkling tease,
Cracking up the universe with ease.

Starry-Eyed Jokes

Twinkle, twinkle, little star,
Your dad's a gas—what a bizarre!
While meteors fall, they trip on light,
Slipping on rockets, what a sight!

Asteroids roll with jests so bold,
Galactic giggles never grow old.
Supernovae burst in fits of glee,
As aliens chuckle in zero gravity.

Signals from the Stars

Echos from stars bring tales of jest,
Cosmic whispers, at their best.
"Did you hear about the black dwarf?"
"Too dense for jokes, so off he scoffed!"

Messages shoot from light-years away,
A stellar punchline brightens the day.
Gravity waves shake from laughter's might,
As space-time bends with sheer delight.

Abundant Astrological Antics

Zodiac signs plotting their tricks,
Under the moon, with cunning clicks.
A ram's too stubborn, a fish just swims,
While a lion roars at all his whims.

The planets dance in a playful round,
Mercury quips as it spins around.
Venus winks with mischievous glee,
Jupiter chuckles, "Come laugh with me!"

Starlit Shenanigans

In the night sky, twinkling bright,
Stars play jokes that feel just right.
The moon laughs at how we glance,
In this cosmic, silly dance.

Galaxies spin with a wink,
While comets zoom, they never sink.
Asteroids chuckle, what a sight,
In their orbit, pure delight.

Space is filled with cheerful sounds,
As laughter echoes round the bounds.
Planets giggle in their flight,
Painting joy in the endless night.

So let's revel in the stars,
And share a laugh like cosmic cars.
In this stellar, merry show,
We find joy wherever we go.

Cosmic Corniness

A starry pun lights up the way,
For every night, there's silly play.
Asteroids roll with grin so wide,
In this universe, we can't hide.

The sun beams down with golden rays,
Spreading jokes in sunny ways.
Galaxies swirl with laughter's glow,
As funny vibes begin to grow.

Aliens giggle at our rhyme,
Making humor out of time.
In the void where shadows creep,
We find the jokes that make us leap.

Out in space, the laughter's loud,
Echoing through the starry crowd.
In this cosmic circus, take a seat,
For humor and joy, it can't be beat.

Exoplanet Exaggerations

Farther out, beyond our sight,
Planets boast with pure delight.
They claim to have the best of pranks,
And tell tall tales with playful janks.

One says it can jump so high,
It tickles comets as they fly.
Another claims to dance and spin,
While black holes wink with a cheeky grin.

Saturn's rings are all a show,
For every twirl, they steal the glow.
Neptune laughs with a bubbling cheer,
While Venus jokes, "I'm the best here!"

In a universe so vast and wide,
Whispers of laughter cannot hide.
So let's join in, unwind the fate,
In the jest of worlds, let's celebrate.

Dark Matter Delights

In shadows deep, where laughter hides,
Dark matter plays where fun abides.
Its mystery brings a smirk and tease,
As secrets float upon the breeze.

Gravity pulls jokes from the air,
While spinning stars create a flare.
Invisible laughs in the night unfold,
With humor that can't be controlled.

Quasars beam with a cheeky grin,
While black holes whisper, "Come on in!"
The cosmos filled with joyous sights,
In the dance of dark, our hearts take flights.

So listen closely to the space,
Where giggles echo in endless chase.
In every corner, light may flee,
But joy survives eternally.

Atmosphere of Amusement

In orbit around a quirky star,
The laughter echoes from afar.
Planets spin with giggles bright,
While comets dance in sheer delight.

Jupiter's storms are quite a show,
As moons join in the jesting flow.
Saturn's rings, they joke and sway,
Creating smiles that light the way.

A laugh from Mars, a chuckle from Earth,
In this zone of cosmic mirth.
Galaxies twist in playful spins,
Where even dark matter grins.

Gravity's pull has lost its grip,
As humor takes a joyful trip.
Within the vast, serene expanse,
The universe joins this silly dance.

Nebulae of Nonsense

In a cloud where thoughts collide,
Nonsense reigns with stellar pride.
Stars giggle as they form and twirl,
Spinning tales in a cosmic whirl.

A funny joke from a shooting star,
Bright enough to catch a spar.
Supernova laughs ignite the night,
With cosmic jokes that feel just right.

From distant realms, the laughter flies,
Wobbling planets in the skies.
Nebulae burst with comic relief,
Bringing joy beyond belief.

In the chaos of cosmic play,
All the stars play tag each day.
With every twinkle, laughter blooms,
As nonsense fills the silent rooms.

Stellar Shenanigans

The Milky Way plays peek-a-boo,
With constellations drawn anew.
Stars twinkle with a cheeky grin,
As comets come and whirl within.

Orion cracks a clever jest,
While Venus starts a cosmic fest.
Planets giggle in their dance,
As asteroids join in the prance.

Light-years stretch with giddy glee,
Spreading joy through infinity.
In the void where echoes teem,
Astrophysics takes a playful theme.

From quasars bright to black holes tight,
Every galaxy shines so bright.
With shenanigans that never cease,
The cosmos whispers laughter's peace.

Chortles of the Cosmos

In the vastness where starlights beam,
The universe giggles in a dream.
Among the moons, a joke is told,
As constellations shimmer bold.

A black hole sighs with a funny fable,
Creating smiles at every table.
Distant worlds with chuckles rife,
As laughter dances through all life.

With echoes of glee, planets collide,
While cosmic winds swirl with pride.
Each supernova flickers cheer,
Spreading humor far and near.

Galaxies twirl in whimsical grace,
As joy lights up the endless space.
With stellar delight around each bend,
The cosmos laughs, and will not end.

Orbiting Humor

In space where laughter swirls around,
Asteroids tumble, humor's found.
Galaxies giggle, stars do delight,
As comets dance in the cosmic night.

Nebulas whisper jokes to the stars,
Shooting meteors play on guitars.
Gravity pulls at our cheeky grin,
In the vast expanse, we all fit in.

Planets rotate with a chuckling sound,
While space dust scatters laughter around.
A cosmic joke, a stellar tease,
In the universe, we find our ease.

Spaceships cruise in a merry spree,
Where humor floats, wild and free.
With every orbit, joy takes flight,
Creating smiles in the endless night.

Planetary Puns

Mercury's quick with a witty retort,
While Venus shines bright in the fun-filled court.
Earth's got a joke about its own dirt,
And Mars claims it's the best at dessert.

Jupiter's storms burst with laughter's sound,
Saturn rolls with rings that astound.
Uranus giggles, oh what a sight,
While Neptune dances under the light.

Pluto shimmies with a charming flair,
Where all the planets love to share.
In this cosmic class, jesters abound,
With every rotation, more fun is found.

Comet Comedy

A comet streaks with a tail so bright,
Telling jokes that soar through the night.
It zips past moons, side-splitting glee,
As laughter echoes in the galaxy.

With a wink and a whirl, it delivers its jest,
Crashing through silence, it's truly the best.
A comic star in an endless chase,
Leaving trails of joy in outer space.

As it hurtles on, it gathers the cheer,
Sharing cosmic giggles far and near.
With each joyful burst, a heavenly spree,
Making the universe bright and free.

Asteroid Amusement

Asteroids bounce with a playful jig,
Bumping into each other, it's quite the gig.
Their rocky forms roll with mirthful cheer,
Creating laughter for all to hear.

In this celestial dance, they swing and sway,
Telling tales of fun in their own way.
Each collision sparks a joke so grand,
In the vastness where humor takes a stand.

With each orbit, their mischief grows,
Witty remarks in their rocky throes.
A merry band floating far from Earth,
In the cosmos, they find their worth.

Lunar Laughs

On the moon, cheese wheels roll,
A crater's a snack, oh how they stroll.
Astronauts giggle, they can't help but grin,
For every small step ends with a spin.

Rockets drive like cars, taking a flight,
But the gas bill is quite the sight!
Comets tailgate, wanting a race,
Yet space is just one big, open space.

Stars twinkle with humor, they'll shine
While galaxies play games, oh so divine.
Asteroids chuckle, they bounce on their trails,
Each one a jest in the cosmic tales.

In weightlessness, jokes just float,
Like silly dreams on a spacecraft boat.
With every orbit, laughter will rise,
The universe winks with wise little eyes.

Satellite Satire

Satellites spin, like tops they whirl,
Catching signals in a dizzy swirl.
They beam down jokes from outer space,
With notes that tickle, oh what a race!

Orbits get tangled, a cosmic knot,
Planets gossip, they talk a lot.
Mars made a joke, Venus turned red,
And Earth rolled its eyes, 'You're not that clever,' it said.

In the Milky Way, fun reigns supreme,
While comets laugh, like they're in a dream.
Uranus chuckles at the stories told,
Of space mishaps and treasures of old.

Gravity pulls, but spirit stays light,
As asteroids tumble, what a delight!
Across the heavens, the joy does glide,
For laughter's migration knows no divide.

Supernova Satires

Stars go supernova, bursting with flair,
Exploding with laughter, spreading everywhere.
Their twinkling giggles, a cosmic delight,
They light up the sky in the deep, dark night.

Black holes mumble jokes, deep and profound,
While nebulas swirl, their laughter unbound.
Galaxies spin tales with a twist,
An interstellar stand-up, you just can't miss!

Each light-year traveled, a punchline unfolds,
In the great vastness, the humor never grows old.
Time expands, but the fun just speeds,
In the universe's heart, joy is what it feeds.

Nova orbits weave, a tapestry bright,
With humor entwined through the stars' endless flight.
The cosmos erupts in a joyous spree,
Even in darkness, we chuckle with glee!

Gravity Grins

On Earth we trip, and we often fall,
But zero-gravity brings giggles to all.
Floating snacks tease, they dance in the air,
Like sugar-coated whispers that giggle and flare.

Cosmic slides send astronauts in spins,
While weightlessness brings out our silly grins.
Rocket rides jostle, it's a wild show,
Bumping and bouncing, where else could we go?

Planets align for a whimsical game,
Where each little quirk is worthy of fame.
The sun beamed brightly, made shadows ballet,
And the moon laughed out loud, "I'm here to stay!"

The pull of the cosmos, it tugs at our hearts,
As laughs and glee play their cheerful parts.
With every orbit, the joy takes flight,
In the fabric of space, we dance with delight!

Nebulous Natter

In the vastness where echoes play,
Stars whisper jokes in a cosmic ballet.
Planets chuckle, asteroids giggle,
Galaxies spin in a playful wiggle.

A comet's tail wags like a pup,
While Saturn rings flip, joking up.
Venus rolls her eyes, it's no surprise,
Even the moons can't resist the cries.

Uranus bursts forth with a punny line,
Jupiter's storms are just mood divine.
Black holes yawn, in a void of glee,
Space is a joke, come laugh with me!

So drift through this laughter-filled space,
Where humor hides in every place.
Join the fun, don't be a snooze,
In this galactic realm, you can't lose!

Comedic Constellations

Orion forgot his belt tonight,
Shooting stars flash in comedic light.
Ursa Major cracks a beary old joke,
While Canis Minor waits for the poke.

Twinkling stars twirl in punny delight,
As constellations dance in the night.
Draco's tail flicks with endless wit,
Even the Milky Way can't quit!

Pegasus neighs, 'Is this a hitch?'
And Virgo replies, 'I'm just a glitch!'
Laughter rings out like celestial bells,
As the universe spins and giggles swell.

So gaze at the sky, let joy unfold,
In the arms of humor, let your heart be bold.
For in this realm of cosmic play,
Laughter unites in a starry ballet!

Starship Satire

On a ship sailing through the starlit sea,
Captain Quip jokes, 'Aren't we all free?'
Asteroids float, all decked in flair,
While the crew busts jokes, light as air.

'What's a star's favorite beverage?' they cheer,
'The Milky Way's milkshake, it's always near!'
Warp drives hum with a rhythmic beat,
As laughter fills every corner and seat.

Navigating through punchlines, oh so bright,
Exploring the cosmos, fueled by delight.
Time bends and twists under the punny reign,
In humor's embrace, there's no room for pain.

So hop on board, leave worry behind,
In the corridors of jest, happiness you'll find.
Starship floating, let the giggles ignite,
In galactic wonder, we soar through the night!

Whimsical Worlds

In a land where the stars wear hats so bright,
Planets parade through the shimmering night.
A universe filled with whimsical sight,
Each corner alive with giggles and light.

Venus dashes by in her comet fast,
While Mars cracks a joke from the cosmic past.
Pluto sighs, 'At least I'm not alone,'
In this ballet of laughter, we all have grown.

Galaxies gurgle with bubbles of mirth,
Stardust dances, knowing its worth.
Earth chuckles round, as moonbeams align,
Each twinkle a testament to joy's design.

So spin through these worlds, so merry and wise,
With every twirl, let humor arise.
In this realm of the bizarre and fun,
Our laughter extends, like the light of the sun!

Astrological Antics

In the sky, they spin and dance,
Stars with a twinkle, a cosmic chance.
Jupiter's gas, a bloated sight,
Calls for a laugh on a moonlit night.

Saturn's rings, a colorful show,
Wonders if it's just a hula-hoop glow.
Venus teases with beauty so bright,
Winks at Mars in the soft starlight.

Uranus giggles, a quirky breeze,
While Neptune whistles with cosmic ease.
Asteroids toss, in a playful race,
Playing tag through the vast open space.

Meteoric Mirth

A comet streaks by, a wink and a grin,
Shooting stars shriek, 'Let the fun begin!'
In this celestial parade of sheer delight,
Galaxies laugh in the deep, starry night.

The moon whispers jokes to the sun up high,
While the Milky Way winks with a twinkling eye.
Mars spins around, a cheeky red lad,
Saying, 'I'm not just a planet, I'm cosmic rad!'

With space dust confetti, they dance with cheer,
Every twinkle and glow, a giggle, my dear.
In orbits they frolic, no troubles in sight,
Just laughter and joy in the infinite light.

Tidal Teasers

Oceans ripple under starlit beams,
Waves laugh and tease like whimsical dreams.
Tides play peek-a-boo, dipping and rising,
Whispering secrets, surprisingly surprising.

The sun, a joker, pulls the sea's strings,
With moonlit giggles, each wave brightly sings.
From crests to troughs, they splash and they flow,
Turning the shore to a bubbly show.

Seagulls discuss where the next joke will land,
Chasing each other in a soft, sandy strand.
The ocean's punchline, a splashy embrace,
Life's funny at tides, dancing with grace.

Cosmic Cracks

In the expanse where the galaxies twirl,
Quasars crack jokes that make light whirl.
Black holes are shy, but when they engage,
Spinning fun tales from their dark, secret stage.

Solar flares burst with a sudden laugh,
While constellations share their cosmic graph.
Pluto rolls by, a dwarf with a grin,
Saying, 'I might be small, but I still fit in!'

Astro-antics in a boundless spree,
Every star knows the punchline, you see.
In the fabric of space where humor's unbound,
Cosmic cracks echo with joy all around.

Martian Mischief

In red dust, the Martians play,
With green cheese they throw all day.
A rover tripped and took a fall,
"That's one small step, not so small!"

They giggle from behind a rock,
With clever tricks they always shock.
Hop on one leg, then spin around,
Their laughter echoes, a joyful sound.

A UFO zooms, they pull a fast one,
"Look at that, we've roped the sun!"
Orange rays, they poke and tease,
In their fun, the cosmos freeze.

Martians dance to a twinkling tune,
Underneath their playful moon.
With every giggle, the stars align,
In Martian mischief, all is fine.

Jovian Jests

On Jupiter's clouds, the jokers thrive,
With storms of laughter, they come alive.
Gas giants rumble in playful cheer,
While the moons spin tales, crystal clear.

They pull pranks with a booming shout,
"Look, a comet! What's that about?"
Saturn laughs with rings that sway,
While Jovians bumble in a playful ballet.

"Is it windy, or are you just gassy?"
They ponder jokes that sound quite classy.
Floating high, they share their jest,
Creating smiles across the fest.

Jovian jests echo far and wide,
Through swirling storms, their humor's tied.
With every chuckle, the heavens gleam,
In the giant's realm, it's a cosmic dream.

Orbital Chuckles

In a space loop where smiles ignite,
Orbiting planets share giggles at night.
A satellite spins with a witty claim,
"I just want to be the star of the game!"

Asteroids tumble, a rocky ballet,
Whispering jokes that float away.
"Why did the comet break up?" they cry,
"It needed space, don't ask me why!"

Around the sun, they dance in flight,
Planetary humor is outta sight.
Jokes fly high on a solar breeze,
In this cosmic love, they find their ease.

Orbital chuckles weave through the sky,
As laughter ignites the stars nearby.
With every jest, the galaxies swirl,
In this vast play, the cosmos unfurl.

Space Oddities

In the void, there's laughter galore,
Space oddities tumble and soar.
A nebula blushes, a star goes bold,
"I'm the sun's favorite – or so I'm told!"

Black holes wink, pulling light from the past,
Creating jokes that forever last.
"What's a spaceship's favorite drink?" they smirk,
"Gravity's punch – it really works!"

A cosmic clown with a twinkling grin,
Sells vacuum treats made of pure spin.
"Step right up, it's a stellar hoot!
Star dust candy, it's quite a loot!"

With every quirk, the universe beams,
In this oddity dance, we live our dreams.
Space oddities laugh under starlit skies,
As we gaze up in wonder, with wide-open eyes.

Galactic Giggles

In the depths of space, stars twinkle bright,
Planets spin on jokes, what a sight!
A comet zooms past with a wink and a grin,
Even black holes laugh at the fun they spin.

Asteroids crack up in their rocky dance,
While a sunbeam winks, giving moons a chance.
Galaxies rotate in cosmic delight,
Each light-year traveled brings humor in sight.

Saturn's rings jingle in a playful tune,
Dancing around while they float under the moon.
Mars tells a story of a sweet, silly fight,
All the creatures giggle in the gentle night.

So if you float near the Milky Way's fold,
Tune in for laughter, in stories retold.
For in this universe, joy takes the lead,
Comedy sprouts like a funny little seed.

Interstellar Wit

In the vacuum of space, where whispers abound,
Echos of laughter can easily be found.
A Martian with jokes flows like water in streams,
While the Saturnian jester plots wondrous schemes.

Twinkling stars chuckle, they say it's a blast,
As light-years of punchlines swirl round them fast.
Even the moons join in with a chuckle or two,
Casting shadows of gags that seem ever so new.

With planets that spin, and comets that race,
Galactic humor lights up the cold space.
A spacecraft sails by with a witty remark,
As laughter ignites in the dark of the arc.

So here's to the cosmos that tickles our minds,
With whims that are wacky and laughter that binds.
In the vastness of night, don't forget to explore,
The whimsical wonders of humor galore.

Celestial Quips

Orbiting worlds where jesters reside,
Uranus snickers, it's quite the wild ride.
While Venus is laughing, it's hot as the sun,
With jokes that erupt, oh, it's such heavenly fun!

And if you should visit the rings of the king,
You'll find Saturn's antics just make your heart sing.
Mercury's quick, with a quip up its sleeve,
Sharing giggles faster than you can believe.

Nebulae gather to share their best puns,
Creating a space that just bursts with good runs.
While light years drift by with no limit in sight,
A universe filled with comedic delight.

So let's toast to the laughter that twinkles and glows,
In every nook of the sky where humor flows.
For cosmic comedians are here to stay strong,
With celestial quips that make everything wrong.

Nebula Nonsense

In a cloud of bright colors, a laughter is spun,
With stars in their eyes, they're just having some fun.
A silly old quasar spits jokes like confetti,
And wormholes invite us to join in the jetty.

From comets to quasars, the humor takes flight,
With cosmic slip-ups that shine in the night.
Grab your space suit, we're in for a jest,
The universe winks, oh, isn't it blessed?

Galactic giggles echo through time,
Asteroids chuckling in rhythm and rhyme.
The dance of the cosmos brings laughter anew,
In every dark corner, joy breaks on through.

So let's join the laughter and spread it like spice,
For in nebula nonsense, life feels so nice.
Every planet around has a story to share,
With funny little tales that float through the air.

Light-Speed Laughs

A comet raced by, just a blur,
"Hey, slow down!" said the meteor.
"I can't help it!" the comet grinned,
"I'm just here for a cosmic spin!"

Stars twinkled bright with a wink,
"Don't trip over the Milky's sink!"
A black hole laughed in a gravity bind,
"Guess I'm the center, never maligned!"

Mars looked down at his rusty hue,
"Red's the new black, don't you think too?"
Venus sighed, line drawn in the sand,
"At least I'm hot; you still can't stand!"

With light-speed laughter in their race,
Asteroids chuckled in endless space.
The universe spun with each silly jest,
In the galaxy's heart, we're all really blessed!

Saturn's Silliness

Saturn wore rings, shining so grand,
"I'm the bling-bling of this whole band!"
Uranus rolled his eyes with flair,
"Too much style, not a care in the air!"

Jupiter joked, "You're looking too tight!"
"Better support, or you might just fight!"
Saturn replied with a twinkling smile,
"I'm just here to make space worth your while!"

Moons twirled round in a merry dance,
"Join us now, come take a chance!"
With laughter echoing through the skies,
Even the asteroids sighed with surprise.

In this ringed wonder of humor bright,
The laughter soared through the cosmic night.
Funny and playful, they shared a cheer,
Silliness reigns when the planets are near!

Orbital Oddities

A satellite tripped on a wire,
"Why so tense? Are you late to expire?"
The planets giggled, caught in the spin,
"Don't get too caught up in the din!"

Neptune laughed with bubbles afloat,
"Caught in a whirlpool, don't rock the boat!"
Mercury zoomed with a mischievous gleam,
"Catch me if you can, I'm the fastest dream!"

Comets played tag, zipping in flight,
"Last one back is a black hole's fright!"
Jokes flew like meteors blazing bright,
Quantum giggles filled the cold night.

In this odd dance of orbital cheer,
Every twinkle held a story dear.
The universe laughed with a cosmic shout,
Finding joy in the unexpected rout!

Celestial Chuckles

In the cosmos, a star made a jest,
"Why don't aliens ever rest?"
"Because they're always on a probe!"
"Best way to discover the galactic globe!"

A small moon winked at its planet friend,
"Why so blue, when you've got a blend?"
"Because they call me the cold little ball!"
"You are the glitter, you shine for us all!"

The sun beamed warm, with a playful tease,
"I'll burn your jokes; they're easy to freeze!"
A planet replied, rolling its rings,
"But your light can't dim what laughter brings!"

In each twinkle, a giggle was found,
Across the universe, joy danced around.
With every chuckle shared up high,
The celestial realms filled with laughter in the sky!

Martian Mirth

On Mars, they say the cheese is best,
A slice of galaxy, a tasty quest.
Alien diners munch with glee,
Sipping on stars, a cosmic spree.

Red dust swirls as laughter flows,
In craters deep, where humor glows.
With every laugh, the Martians beam,
Creating joy in their spacey dream.

Jovian Jests

Jupiter's storms create a fuss,
But in the clouds, they ride a bus.
Each lightning flash a punchline flies,
Witty whispers in thunderous skies.

Around the moons, they joke and tease,
With gas giant laughter that never leaves.
A funny dance in swirling air,
Where joy expands, no need to spare.

Saturn's Satire

Rings of laughter twirl through space,
In Saturn's realm, there's no disgrace.
The icy bands, they shine and gleam,
As humor flows like a celestial stream.

With each rotation, chuckles rise,
Jokes spiral up to starlit skies.
In cosmic swings, they take a chance,
Twisting wit in a playful dance.

Eclipse of Laughter

When moon obscures the sun's bright light,
Eclipsed in joys, the night feels right.
Space giggles chase the shadows away,
In the dark, all creatures play.

A comet's tail can tickle your nose,
While starlight sparkles as humor grows.
In the quiet of the universe so wide,
Laughter echoes, an endless ride.

Cosmic Caper Chronicles

In a galaxy far with a quirky jest,
Planets spin round, each does its best.
Stars wink and twinkle, a humorous sight,
Orbiting laughter that dances in light.

Comets zoom by with a funny tail,
Telling tales of space with a cosmic trail.
Black holes chuckle, they've got the scoop,
Swallowing quirks in a galactic loop.

Rockets blast off with a bouncy cheer,
Fuelled by puns that we hold dear.
Asteroids giggle as they dance on track,
In the vastness, joy finds no lack.

So grab your gear, the trip's begun,
With laughter and jokes, it'll be some fun.
From stars to moons, we'll share a grin,
In the boundless space, let the laughter begin!

Galactic Gags

Floating in space, a joke hits home,
Planets in line, they're ready to roam.
Shooting stars wink with a sparkle bright,
While Martians chuckle at a comical sight.

From Venus to Mars, the laughs take flight,
Every moon beams with pure delight.
Gravity pulls with a playful tease,
As astronauts giggle and do as they please.

In the cosmic dance, the starlight plays,
Twinkling laughter through endless days.
Supernova bursts with a pop and a flare,
Creating humor that's beyond compare.

So gather 'round, let the stories unfold,
In the universe vast, let your spirit be bold.
With every tick of the cosmic clock,
We'll share a laugh, around the rock!

Jovial Journeys

Rocketing through space, a whimsical ride,
With laughter and joy, we bounce side to side.
Galaxies spin in a playful embrace,
Every turn holds a grin on our face.

Stardust sprinkles a magical mood,
While aliens dance to a merry tune brewed.
Nebulas burst with colors so bright,
Bringing giggles and chuckles into the night.

Space whales sing with a glorious tone,
In this cosmic realm, we are never alone.
With comical sights beyond our wild dreams,
We laugh and we joke, or so it seems.

So journey with me through the Milky Way,
With humor and fun, we'll laugh all day.
In the realms of stars, joy knows no bounds,
In the heart of the cosmos, laughter resounds!

Out of This World Humor

Beyond the blue, where the cosmos glow,
Where laughter erupts like a meteoric show.
Galactic jesters, with tricks up their sleeves,
Spreading their cheer, like autumn leaves.

Stars gather round for a comedy night,
With cosmic punchlines that feel just right.
Saturn spins jokes as it twirls its ring,
While asteroids laugh and join in to sing.

Each planet's a player, each moon's a cheer,
With humor that seems to float in the sphere.
In the fabric of space, we weave with glee,
As every joke rockets wild and free.

So lift off today on a humor spree,
In the universe vast, come laugh with me.
For in outer space, the joy is absurd,
In the laughter of stars, let your heart be stirred!

Asteroid Antics

Asteroids roll in a cosmic dance,
They trip and tumble, not left to chance.
They juggle rocks in their vast ballet,
All the while, making space their play.

One bumps a planet, oh what a scene!
'You rock my world!' says the clumsy green.
While meteorites mete out their fates,
Orbiting friends giggle as it creates.

With rings of Saturn, they form a band,
Playing tunes that are simply unplanned.
'Out of this world!' shouts a satellite,
Laughter echoes through the starry night.

Gravity's not too heavy tonight,
Floating with joy in the infinite light.
As they zoom past, they flick and toss,
In the vastness of space, they're the boss.

Quirky Quasars

Quasars shine with a radiant beam,
Filling the cosmos like a wild dream.
They're light-years ahead on the cosmic stage,
Flipping out jokes from the galaxy's page.

One whispers, 'You light up my sky!'
While spinning tales as they drift by.
Another quips, 'I'm super unique!'
Laughing loudly, they start to squeak.

With a twinkle and wink, they play tag,
Adventure awaits, waving a flag.
In their raucous jaunt through the vastness wide,
They jive with the stars, taking all in stride.

So if you gaze into that starry swirl,
Remember the humor of the cosmic whirl.
For even in space, where the time is odd,
Laughter floats free—oh, how it's broad!

Comet Capers

Comets come in with a brilliant tail,
Shooting across the night without fail.
They're the jesters of the astral show,
Bringing giggles as they brightly glow.

One exclaims, 'I'm on a streak!'
With a dazzling curve, they strongly speak.
Another comets back, 'Don't be shy!'
In this splendid show, let's all fly high.

With a flick and a wink, they zip and zoom,
Their paths a joyful, shimmering plume.
When they pass, the planets cheer,
'Catch you later, dear comet, my dear!'

They share their tales of spacey glee,
A skateboard ride through infinity.
So when you spot that cosmic shape,
Join the giddy laughter, make no escape!

Nebula Nonsense

Nebulas swirl in a colorful dream,
Painting galaxies with a vibrant scheme.
They giggle as they puff and sigh,
Forming shapes that are out to defy.

One morphs into a silly cat,
While another changes to a big old hat.
'Look at me!' calls a starry sprout,
In this funny realm, there's no doubt.

They twist and turn, bouncing about,
Tickling each other with a cosmic shout.
Stars blink in rhythm to their delight,
Creating joy through the endless night.

So next time you peek at the sky's embrace,
Know that laughter is written in space.
In the heart of the cosmos, where all dreams play,
Nonsense thrives in a whimsical way.

Cosmic Comedy Showdown

In a galaxy far, far away,
The stars twinkle and play.
A comet cracks a joke,
Leaving asteroids to poke.

Quasars laugh at black holes,
While satellites spin like trolls.
Gravity pulls on the joke tight,
As laughter echoes through the night.

Nebulas are giggling bright,
While space dust dances in flight.
Even the moons start to chuckle,
As comets plot their quirk and hustle.

In this cosmic comedy spree,
Nothing's too odd or silly.
With each punchline, stardust gleams,
It's a laughter-filled space dream.

Universal Banter

Stars and planets had a chat,
Even the sun wore a hat.
Mercury winks with a grin,
As Venus joins in for the win.

The moons throw a playful fight,
While asteroids tumble with delight.
Jupiter boasts of its size,
While Saturn just twirls, oh so spry.

They share their tales in cosmic rhyme,
Rockets zoom by, what's the time?
Galactic giggles fill the air,
While aliens swing in a funny affair.

Across the void, laughter rolls,
As comets barge in with their strolls.
In the universe, joy's the game,
Every chuckle has no shame.

Lattice of Laughs

Built in orbits, laughter weaves,
Through trails of stardust leaves.
Stars connect with light so bold,
Creating stories yet untold.

A laugh echoes from red dwarf,
As galaxies twist and morph.
Even a black hole can share,
Absurdities beyond compare.

From the edge of space, jokes collide,
Each planet hosts a quirky side.
Supernova's bright spark ignites,
As cosmic beings reach new heights.

In this lattice, fun expands,
Across the void, where joy stands.
No celestial body is immune,
To the sweet laughter of the moon.

Cosmic Idiosyncrasies

Venus with her hats so bright,
Dances with Martians all night.
Pluto winks, a bit shy and cute,
While Saturn's rings start to hoot.

A star sneezes, come take a look,
As Milky Way reads a funny book.
Uranus giggles, takes a spin,
In this cosmic contest, who'll win?

Wormholes twist with a chuckle,
As timelines warp, time to snuggle.
Across the cosmos, they play so fair,
Finding oddities everywhere.

With every quirk, they set the pace,
In the vastness of space, they embrace.
In this universe of silly spree,
Cosmic idiosyncrasies make us glee.

Milky Way Wit

In a galaxy far, jokes do unfold,
Stars share giggles, gleaming and bold.
Asteroids chuckle, comets take flight,
Laughter erupts in the deep, dark night.

Planets spin tales of cosmic delight,
Venus trips over, lost in her flight.
Jupiter's jokes are gigantic in size,
While Mars gets the pun, but rarely the prize.

Solar winds whisper, puns in the breeze,
Shooting stars dance with effortless ease.
Each planet a player in this comedy play,
In the vastness of space, they giggle away.

So if you're stargazing, just look up above,
The universe teems with laughter and love.
The Milky Way shines, not just a display,
With humor that travels light-years away.

Laughter in the Cosmos

In the void of space where silence reigns,
Laughter echoes through interstellar lanes.
Galaxies twirl in a dance of glee,
Winking at earthlings, just wait and see.

Nebulae burst with colorful fun,
As star clusters giggle, 'Aren't we the one?'
Saturn's rings jingle like tunes on a spree,
While meteors race with wild jubilee.

Black holes laugh at the jokes that they catch,
Pulling in punchlines, but never a match.
Cosmic rays tickle the vastness of space,
Inviting all mortals to laugh in their place.

So join in the fun, let your spirits fly,
Where laughter is light, and the stars are the sky.
The cosmos is chuckling, don't let it wait,
Find humor in orbits that glitter and sate.

Quasar Quirks

Quasars shine bright with a peculiar glow,
Cracking up space, where the mysteries flow.
With a wink and a nod, they twist and they spin,
Leaving behind trails of quirkiness win.

With energy fierce, they spark and ignite,
Creating chuckles that pierce through the night.
Cosmic comedians, they know how to play,
Turning shadows to laughter in a quirky display.

Each light-year a punchline, each beam quite a jest,
In the theater of night, they're simply the best.
So if you're feeling low, just glance at the stars,
The universe thrives on its luminous bars.

Join in the fun, let your worries all part,
For the quirks of a quasar can lighten the heart.
As stardust and laughter dance hand in hand,
We find joy in the cosmos, so grand and so planned.

Pluto's Punchlines

In the cold of the night, little Pluto does grin,
Crafting quick punchlines as if it's a win.
Though a dwarf amongst giants, it holds its own sway,
Tickling the fancies of all who come play.

With icy remarks that chill to the core,
It jokes about size, yet still asks for more.
Its heart-shaped crater's a laugh in disguise,
Winking at earthlings under those vast skies.

Orbiting far in a solar retreat,
Pluto shares giggles, so warm and so sweet.
Ghostly and distant, it sings to the night,
Spreading joy through the darkness, a true galactic light.

So embrace the delight that this world has to share,
With Pluto's own punchlines in the cool cosmic air.
For laughter transcends every boundary, every hue,
Binding us together in moments anew.

Meteoric Mirth

Why did the comet cross the sky?
To leave his tail and wave goodbye!
Stars snickered as he flew so bright,
While asteroids danced in sheer delight.

A rocket asked, 'Why such a rush?'
The comet said, 'I'm in a hush!'
An alien laughed, 'What's the plan?'
'Just shooting for a cosmic span!'

A moonbeam winked and twirled with glee,
'Your humor's out of this galaxy!'
With every joke, the stardust swirled,
A joyful laugh from a twinkling world.

So when you gaze at the vast night sky,
Remember the jokes that soar and fly!
In the laughter of space, find your flight,
For joy is the true star in the night.

Punchlines from the Planets

Why did Mars break up with Venus?
He found her too close to the genius!
Jupiter laughed, 'That's quite a scene!'
'Sometimes love's not so serene.'

Saturn shrugged, rings gleaming bright,
'What do you call a planet that's polite?'
'Urans!' one moon chimed with a grin,
'The jokes keep spinning, let's begin!'

'If Earth is round, then tell me how,
Can logic live where rivers bow?'
The planets giggled, swirling near,
Each punchline spun through cosmic cheer!

So let's toast to orbs that play,
With laughter echoing every day!
For in the cosmos, far and wide,
Humor's the best celestial guide.

Whimsical Whirlwinds

What do you call a storm in space?
A whirlwind dance with a funny face!
Stars twinkled at each swirling tease,
As galaxies chuckled in the breeze.

'A nebula's joke is out of sight,'
Said a starfish star on a chilly night.
'Why did the satellite break his vow?
He just couldn't find a one-liner now!'

Comets raced, leaving trails so fine,
'They call me speedy, but I'm on time!'
With every spin of this cosmic show,
The laughter echoed, 'Just let it flow!'

In the winds of whimsy, take your flight,
With every chuckle, the stars burn bright.
For joy's a gale that sweeps the dark,
Creating laughter, a celestial spark.

Laughter at Light Speed

Why was the rocket feeling blue?
He couldn't find a crew with a view!
The planets laughed and played their role,
'Time for a blast to boost your soul!'

Zooming past at a zany pace,
Light beams danced in a giddy race.
A meteor hollered, 'Don't you fret,
With friends aboard, you'll be all set!'

From Venus to Neptune, jokes took flight,
Each cosmic laugh was pure delight.
In the vast expanse where dreams are spun,
Laughter at light speed is truly fun!

So if you feel lost in the cosmic sweep,
Just tune to the stars, and take a leap.
For in the universe, laughter's the key,
Unlocking joy's endless possibility.

Cosmic Quips

In the void, a joke takes flight,
Stars twinkle with delight.
A comet trails a witty line,
Laughter echoes, oh so fine.

Asteroids chuckle as they roll,
Gravity's pull, a playful toll.
Planetary puns, in orbit they sway,
Round and round, they always play.

Black holes laugh, with all their might,
Sucking in humor, day and night.
A supernova's explosive jest,
In the universe, it's the best.

Celestial bodies share a grin,
In the galaxy, we all win.
Witty remarks from ages past,
In the cosmos, they're unsurpassed.

Galactic Giggles

In the Milky Way, a giggle grows,
Among the stars, it's how it flows.
Nebulae burst with laughter bright,
Creating tales of cosmic light.

Starships zoom with cheeky grins,
Spinning yarns of playful spins.
In this vast and endless spree,
Every light-year brings more glee.

Comets crash with a burst of fun,
Chasing each other, they always run.
Galaxies collide in a bubbly dance,
Embracing chaos, with a chance.

Giggles echo through the night,
As asteroids join in the light.
In this cosmic carnival we see,
A festival of humor flies free.

Celestial Wordplay

Stars have stories, woven so bright,
Jokes shimmer in the velvet night.
Space dust whispers, tickling air,
With every pun, we laugh and share.

Orbiting words, a merry chase,
With twists and turns, it sets the pace.
Each planet sings a silly tune,
As the sun smiles and beams a boon.

Wormholes wink with playful glee,
Transporting jokes from sea to sea.
Celestial puzzles, a quirky dance,
Each cosmic riddle a serendipitous chance.

In the cosmos, wordplay ignites,
Creating joy on starry nights.
With every pun, the universe flares,
In laughter, we find the cares.

Stellar Snickers

Comets' tails wag, swishing fast,
Tickling the stars with giggles cast.
In the void, echoes leap and bound,
Cosmic humor resonates all around.

Mercury's jokes are quick and sly,
While Venus grins, lifting spirits high.
The sun's warm chuckle spreads through space,
Illuminating every face.

Galaxies burst with laughter bright,
Supernovae wink in pure delight.
As stardust sprinkles on Earth-bound ears,
Joy travels light-years through our fears.

With each stellar jest, smiles arise,
Bringing happiness to the skies.
In the laughter of the grand design,
We find our place, our hearts align.

www.ingramcontent.com/pod-product-compliance
Lightning Source LLC
Chambersburg PA
CBHW071824160426
43209CB00003B/200